Just One Hornetto

Created by Keith Chapman

First published in Great Britain by HarperCollins Children's Books in 2008

1 3 5 7 9 10 8 6 4 2
ISBN-13: 978-0-00-726535-0

Based on the television series *Fifi and the Flowertots*
and the original script 'Just One Hornetto' by Dave Ingham.
© Chapman Entertainment Limited 2008

Printed and bound in China
Visit Fifi at: www.fifiandtheflowertots.com

Just One Hornetto

HarperCollins *Children's Books*

Fifi had invited all her Flowertot friends to supper. They were finally going to eat her prized tomato! The only thing was, she hadn't picked it yet, and she was going to need some help.

Slugsy was practising his
trumpet playing, but Stingo was
not enjoying it!

"Slugsy," he shouted, "Stop that racket!"
"Ssorry, bosss," said Slugsy, "but I'm not
the only one playing.
Listen to that guitar,
Stingo – it's lovely!"

"Rotten Raspberries," Stingo spluttered. "It's not lovely at all. It's my horrible cousin, Hornetto. What's he doing here?"

"He's coming this way, Bosss," said Slugsy, "I expect he's come to sssee you."

"Huh," said Stingo, grumpily. "Just tell him I'm not at home!"

"Ah, Slugsy," called out Hornetto. "Where
is my wonderful cousin?"
"He, er, he told me to ssay he's not at home,"
blurted out Slugsy.

Fifi and Bumble were wondering what to do about the tomato. "Hmm," said Bumble. "Perhaps we could ask Webby to make us a special net." "Good idea!" said Fifi. "Let's go and ask her now!"

"Why would Hornetto want
to live in Flowertot Garden?"
Stingo was pacing up and down.
"Because he's up to something,"
Stingo spluttered. "And I'm
going to find out what it is!"

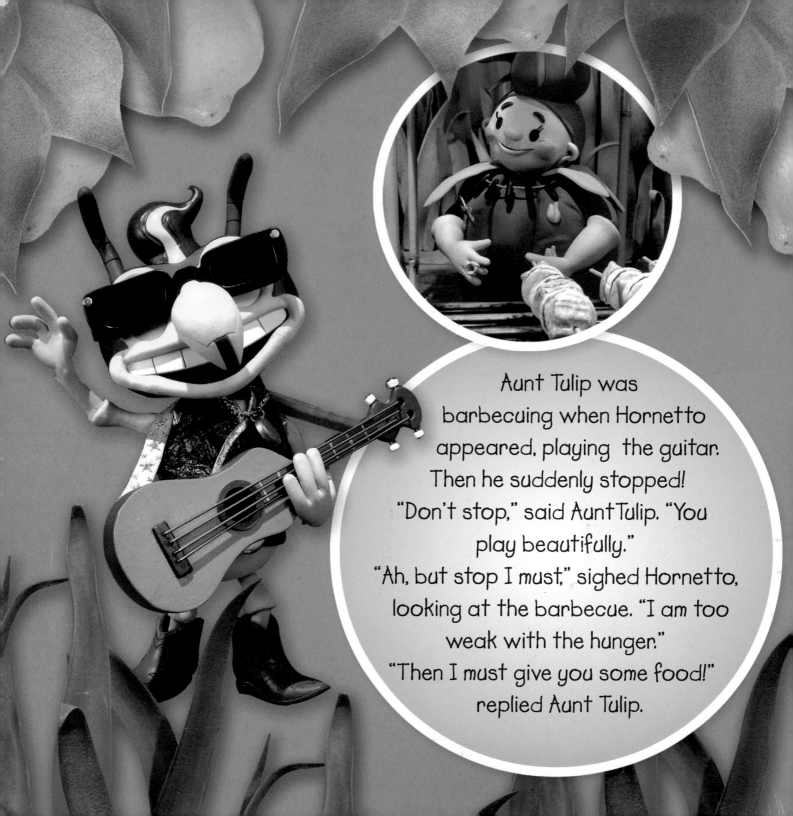

Aunt Tulip was barbecuing when Hornetto appeared, playing the guitar. Then he suddenly stopped!
"Don't stop," said Aunt Tulip. "You play beautifully."
"Ah, but stop I must," sighed Hornetto, looking at the barbecue. "I am too weak with the hunger."
"Then I must give you some food!" replied Aunt Tulip.

Fifi and Bumble followed the music to Poppy's market stall, where Hornetto was entertaining quite a crowd! "What lovely music," said Poppy. "Do have another piece of pie, Hornetto!"

"Ah," grinned Hornetto, as Stingo buzzed into the garden.
"My wonderful cousin! I am so happy to see you!"
"I know what your little game is," Stingo said. "Why don't
you buzz off home and leave me alone?"
"I leave for nobody," answered Hornetto.
"Especially you, stinky Stingo!"

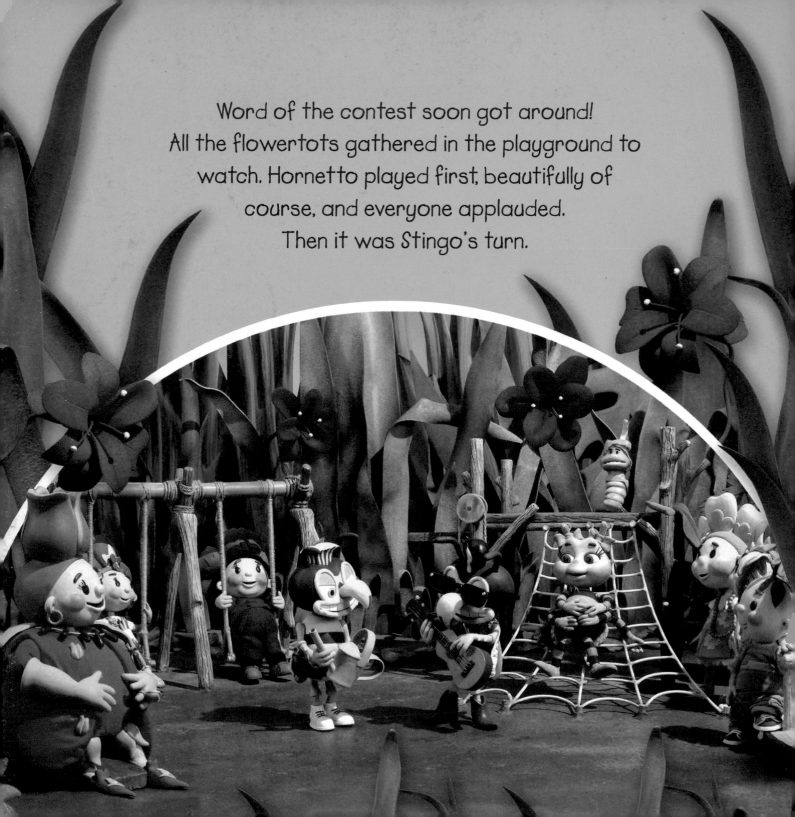

Word of the contest soon got around!
All the flowertots gathered in the playground to
watch. Hornetto played first, beautifully of
course, and everyone applauded.
Then it was Stingo's turn.

"I wonder why Slugsy isn't here to cheer Stingo on," said Fifi.

Stingo put the watering can to his mouth and blew – and everyone was surprised to hear a beautiful sound! But that's because Slugsy was really playing in the bushes!

Hornetto grabbed the
watering can from Stingo's grasp.
But the music didn't stop and
Hornetto knew why. He soon found
Slugsy hiding behind some leaves.

The Flowertots were so surprised.
Stingo looked ashamed.
"Well, I suppose I'd better be going,"
he sniffed.

He might be a naughty wasp, who often made them angry, but they were still sad to see him go.

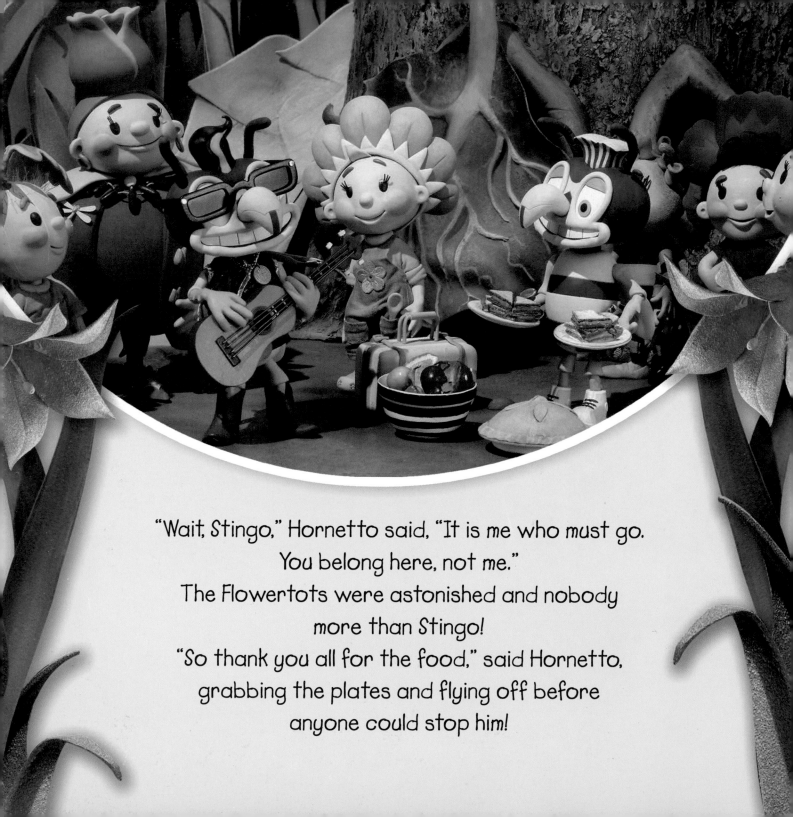

"Wait, Stingo," Hornetto said, "It is me who must go.
You belong here, not me."
The Flowertots were astonished and nobody
more than Stingo!
"So thank you all for the food," said Hornetto,
grabbing the plates and flying off before
anyone could stop him!

Later on Fifi and Bumble got their tomato down safely. Everybody came to Forget-Me-Not Cottage to eat it, including Stingo, who was very happy that he had been allowed to stay!

Make Your Own
Fifi's Fresh Tomato Soup

This chilled soup is a pretty pink colour,
tastes delicious and is really good
for you!

You will need:

* 2 ripe tomatoes
* 1/4 stick celery
* 1 spring onion
* 6 large fresh basil leaves
* 3 tablespoons water

1. Ask an adult to chop the tomatoes and onions, removing the hard tomato centres.

2. Put all the ingredients in a blender and blend until very smooth.

3. Put in the refrigerator to chill before eating.